WHEN RAMADAN IS HERE

Haitham karman

Illustrated by : Lakhaula S. Aulia

Bismillah (In the name of Allah)

Teaching the essence of Islam to kids should be a simple and positive journey. We designed this book with the hope of making it easier to introduce your little family members to their faith and grasp the essence of their religion.

Mommy is in the kitchen, busy with her cooking.

Aaliya is in her playpen, playing with her dolls.

Daddy is in the garden, staring at the sky.

Ali (that's me!) feels that the night is special.

"It's Ramadan," says Mommy.

Ramadan is the ninth month on the Islamic Calendar. Throughout Ramadan, Muslims across the world observe Sawm (fasting), which means that they stop eating and drinking for most of the day.

Since the Islamic Calendar follows the lunar cycle, the sighting of the moon signifies a new Islamic month. This is also why Ramadan always starts ten or eleven days earlier than the previous year.

I join Daddy in the garden.

He's still staring at the night sky.

"There's the moon," Daddy says.

"The moon of Ramadan?" I ask.

"Yes, that's right," Daddy says.

I only fasted a few days last Ramadan, so I can't wait to try again.

Mommy and Daddy always encourage me to do my best.

"Don't worry, Ali! Just fast as much as you can," says Mommy.

Aaliya won't fast because she's still five. Since I am bigger, I will try to fast more this year!

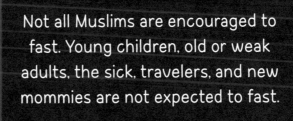

Not all Muslims are encouraged to fast. Young children, old or weak adults, the sick, travelers, and new mommies are not expected to fast.

We wake up before Fajr to have our Suhoor meal.

We break our fast at Maghrib Adhan.

This meal is called Iftar.

We fast from dawn to sunset.

Muslims fast to show Allah how much we love Him. We learn to control our thoughts and actions. Fasting also helps us understand what it is like to be hungry.

"Yes, we do get hungry sometimes, but when we think of why we fast, our hunger will feel less important," says Mommy.

It was during Ramadan that the Quran was first revealed to Prophet Muhammad (PBUH). He was in the Cave of Hira when the Angel Jibreel taught him Surah al-Alaq.

During Ramadan, we recite the Quran more. The Quran was first revealed to our beloved Prophet (PBUH) during Ramadan. I am big enough to recite the Quran. I have memorized a few short Surahs, too. Aaliya is still little, so she's learning the Arabic alphabet.

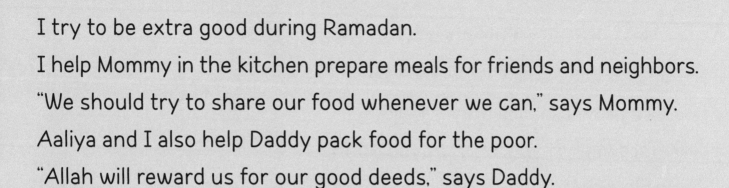

I try to be extra good during Ramadan.

I help Mommy in the kitchen prepare meals for friends and neighbors.

"We should try to share our food whenever we can," says Mommy.

Aaliya and I also help Daddy pack food for the poor.

"Allah will reward us for our good deeds," says Daddy.

Helping others and doing more good deeds than usual is very important in Ramadan. But we should always remember to continue these good deeds in other months as well.

Most days in Ramadan, we visit the mosque after breaking the fast.

We pray a special prayer called Taraweeh that is only prayed during this month.

I meet my friends and neighbors at the mosque.

We pray side by side and give salaams before we leave.

Visiting the mosque during Ramadan is a lot of fun!

Taraweeh is a special prayer performed in Ramadan. It is a long prayer during which Muslims often pray eight units of prayer (although some pray as many as twenty).

Laylat al-Qadr is the night on which the first verses of the Holy Quran were revealed to Prophet Muhammad (PBUH). This night falls on an odd-numbered night within the last ten nights of Ramadan, and a single good deed during this blessed night brings forth the blessings of a thousand months.

The last ten days of Ramadan are extra special.
We go to the mosque without fail.
We recite more Quran.
And we try to do even more good deeds than before.

This is because it could be Laylat al-Qadr.
That's the night on which the Quran was first revealed to Prophet Muhammad (PBUH).

Mommy is in the kitchen making sweets.

Aaliya is on the counter, stirring a bowl of batter.

Daddy is once again in the garden, looking at the sky.

"There's the moon of Shawwal," says Daddy.

Eid Mubarak!

The festival that marks the end of Ramadan falls on the first day of Shawwal. It is called Eid al-Fitr. It's a joyous time during which Muslims get together with friends and family to play games, share meals, and give thanks to Allah.

Having bathed, we wear our best clothes and head to the mosque on Eid.

We go to pray the Eid prayer.

We meet our friends and neighbors as we stand side by side to offer prayers.

All of the children at the mosque (including me and Aaliya!) receive packets of sweets and toys.

On the morning of Eid, Muslims bathe themselves, wear new clothes, apply perfume, and pray Eid Prayers in congregation at the mosque.

We give salaams and wish everyone Eid Mubarak before we leave.

Back at home, we have a feast. Mommy prepared a lot of yummy food last night to enjoy on Eid.

Ramadan is a beautiful and blessed month for Muslims all over the world. Remember the lessons you learned this month for the rest of the year: be kind, share with others, smile, and give thanks to Allah.

Aaliya and I eat too many sweets.
Mommy and Daddy give us Eid gifts, too.
We play, play, and play some more.

We visit friends and neighbors to share our Eid sweets.
We also visit a homeless shelter to provide lunch for everyone there.
"We must not limit our sharing to Ramadan alone. We must continue
to share our blessings with the poor," Mommy says.

Aaliya says she loves sharing.
I love sharing, too!

In the evening, we visit our grandparents.
Our aunts, uncles, and all of our cousins
are there, too.

Grandma and Grandpa prepare
a feast for the whole family.

I eat and play with my cousins until it's time to go home.

I love Eid!

At night, when I lie down in my bed, I peep through the window at the moon.

I am sad that Ramadan is gone.

But Daddy says that Ramadan will be back before I know it.

I can't wait for next Ramadan when I will fast all thirty days, InshaAllah. Ramadan is truly a very special time.

I love Ramadan!

Glossary

Allah   The Arabic word for God

Sawm   The Arabic word for fasting (one of the five pillars of Islam)

Adhan   The Islamic call to prayer

Suhoor   A meal consumed early in the morning before fasting

Iftar   A meal eaten after sunset to break one's fast during Ramadan

Maghrib   The Arabic word for sunset

Quran   The holy book of Islam

Surah   A chapter in the Quran

Eid al-Fitr   A celebration after Ramadan is over

Mubarak   Blessed

RAMADAN MUBARAK

Made in United States
Troutdale, OR
03/08/2024

18292701R00021